Fossilized!
PETRIFIED FORESTS

By Kathleen Connors

Gareth Stevens
Publishing

Please visit our website, www.garethstevens.com. For a free color catalog of all our high-quality books, call toll free 1-800-542-2595 or fax 1-877-542-2596.

Library of Congress Cataloging-in-Publication Data

Connors, Kathleen.
Petrified forests / Kathleen Connors.
    p. cm. — (Fossilized!)
Includes index.
ISBN 978-1-4339-6422-0 (pbk.)
ISBN 978-1-4339-6423-7 (6-pack)
ISBN 978-1-4339-6420-6 (library binding)
1. Petrified forests—Juvenile literature. I. Title.
QE991.C66 2012
561'.16—dc23
                                    2011026247

First Edition

Published in 2013 by
Gareth Stevens Publishing
111 East 14th Street, Suite 349
New York, NY 10003

Copyright © 2013 Gareth Stevens Publishing

Designer: Katelyn E. Reynolds
Editor: Kristen Rajczak

Photo credits: Cover, p. 1 Albert J. Copley/Stockbyte/Getty Images; pp. 4, 9, 10, 11, 17, 20, 21, (cover, pp. 1, 3–24 background and graphics) Shutterstock.com; pp. 5, 15 iStockphoto/Thinkstock; pp. 6–7 Gary Ombler/Dorling Kindersley/ Getty Images; p. 13 Ray Wise/Flickr/Getty Images; p. 14 George Grall/National Geographic/Getty Images; p. 18 Jeff Foott/ Discovery Channel Images/Getty Images; p. 19 Robert F. Sisson/National Geographic/Getty Images.

Printed in the United States of America

CPSIA compliance information: Batch #CW12GS: For further information contact Gareth Stevens, New York, New York at 1-800-542-2595.

CONTENTS

Words in the glossary appear in **bold** type the first time they are used in the text.

FORESTS OF STONE

When is a tree not made of wood? When it's petrified! Some ancient trees petrified, or turned to stone, millions of years ago and left fossils behind. Fossils are the marks or remains of plants and animals. They formed over thousands or millions of years.

Fossilized wood has been found in every part of the United States. Areas with many large pieces of petrified wood are called petrified forests. Today, many petrified forests are national parks.

This is a piece of petrified wood.

This picture of Petrified Forest National Park shows that petrified wood can be both large and small.

▽

FOSSIL WOOD

Fossil wood forms in a few different ways. First, a tree may be buried in **sediment**. The sediment presses down on the wood for many years, keeping it soft and close to the condition it was in when it was buried.

Petrified wood is one kind of fossilized wood. Some petrified wood fossils are **casts**. These form when pieces of wood are quickly buried by sediment and break down. **Minerals** fill the space the wood left and take on its shape.

THE FOSSIL RECORD

Trees that become petrified may have died naturally or been uprooted by a flood or **volcanic eruption.**

Every piece of petrified wood looks different.

PETRIFIED!

Petrified forests are commonly made up of wood petrified by permineralization (puhr-mih-nuh-ruhl-ih-ZAY-shun). Permineralization starts when minerals **dissolved** in water flow into a tree and fill spaces inside and between **cells**. This **preserves** the forms inside the wood.

Petrified forests in the western United States are made of wood permineralized by silica. Millions of years ago, trees were buried in sediment created by volcanic ash that contained the mineral silica. When it mixed with water in the ground, the silica moved into the wood and started the permineralization process.

Petrified wood that has been permineralized by silica, like the wood in this picture, is sometimes called silicified wood.

▽

THE FOSSIL RECORD

Petrified forests can be seen today because the ground shifted over time and lifted up areas where the trees were buried. The sediment and rock covering them wore away.

9

LIKE A RAINBOW

The silica in petrified wood sometimes makes it colorful. Silica becomes quartz, a mineral that forms crystals and changes color based on traces of other minerals in it. If the mineral chromium is present, the wood can even look green! However, some petrified wood still looks like regular logs.

Petrified forests don't look like modern forests. Most of the trees are lying down and have been broken into pieces. They've lost all their branches, leaves, and bark.

◁ Most petrified wood looks like rocks.

Petrified wood is often made into clocks, furniture, jewelry, and objects for decoration.

Not only is petrified wood colorful, it also sparkles in the sunlight.

HOW OLD ARE PETRIFIED FORESTS?

Not all petrified forests are the same age. It depends on when the forests were buried by sediment or a nearby volcano's eruption. For example, a petrified forest in California is about 3.4 million years old, while one in Arizona is more than 211 million years old!

Scientists can figure out how old petrified forests are by studying the rock they were buried in. The older the rock layer, the older the petrified forest.

THE FOSSIL RECORD

Many fossils are found in sedimentary rock, which is formed by sediment being pressed together by natural forces for many years.

The bands of color on the hills behind the petrified tree stump show that sometimes we can see where a rock layer starts and ends.

▽

13

STORIES IN WOOD

Scientists can learn a lot from petrified forests. They compare the cells of fossilized trees to those of modern trees. This helps them figure out when certain kinds of trees began to grow in an area.

Sometimes, petrified wood is used to figure out what an area's **climate** was like millions of years ago. The wood, plus other plant and animal fossils found near it, can tell scientists if an area that's now a desert used to be a forest or a riverbed!

This piece of petrified wood glitters when held up to light.

THE FOSSIL RECORD

Some pieces of petrified wood traveled down waterways for a while. The water made them smooth and rounded. Smaller pieces may look more like pebbles than wood.

Scientists who study petrified wood are called paleobotanists.

15

CONSERVATION

Arizona is home to one of the largest petrified forests in the world. Lorenzo Sitgreaves of the US Army first wrote about the petrified wood in that area in 1851. The wood was so beautiful, many people started to take it. However, **conservationists** wanted to keep the forests safe.

In 1906, some of the area became Petrified Forest National Monument. It was renamed Petrified Forest National Park in 1962 and now takes up an area that covers 146 square miles (378 sq km)!

THE FOSSIL RECORD

Petrified Forest National Park shares some of its land with the Painted Desert. The desert is called "painted" because its rocks and landforms are so colorful.

This picture shows part of Petrified Forest
National Park and a hill in the Painted Desert.

17

PETRIFIED FOREST NATIONAL PARK

The petrified trees that make up the national park in Arizona formed because many trees grew along a river long ago. After the trees died, they floated down the river and got caught together in **logjams**. In time, these logjams became the different "forests" in the park.

Scientists have **identified** about a dozen different kinds of petrified trees in Petrified Forest National Park. They've also found that many of the trees were at least 200 feet (61 m) tall when they were alive!

An ancient logjam became these beautiful petrified wood pieces.

THE FOSSIL RECORD

Some of the famous forests within Petrified Forest National Park are Black Forest, Crystal Forest, and Jasper Forest.

People travel from all over the world to see petrified wood.

MORE PETRIFIED FORESTS

There are many other petrified forests in the United States. Mississippi Petrified Forest was made a National Natural Landmark in 1965. The world's first national park, Yellowstone National Park, also has fossil forests. Fossilized wood has been found in Florida, too.

Petrified forests exist all around the world. One of the most famous petrified forests is Maadi Petrified Forest in Egypt. The fossilized trees there date back 35 million years!

Find petrified forests here!

PETRIFIED
FOREST FACTS

- The logs found in petrified forests often look like someone cut through them with a saw. However, they only look that way because silica always breaks cleanly.

- President Theodore Roosevelt helped set aside the land for Petrified Forest National Monument in 1906.

- The Navajos believed that the trees of Petrified Forest National Park were the bones of a giant named Yiesto.

- It's illegal to take petrified wood from the national parks. However, Petrified Forest National Park reports that visitors steal about a ton of it every month.

Collecting Petrified Wood Prohibited

GLOSSARY

cast: a fossil that is made when a mark or hole left behind by something is filled by minerals

cell: the smallest unit that makes up a living thing

climate: the average weather conditions of a place over a period of time

conservationist: a person concerned with conservation, or the care of nature

dissolve: to mix completely into a liquid

identify: to find out the name or features of something

logjam: a group of logs stuck together in a waterway

mineral: matter found in nature that is not living

preserve: to keep safe

sediment: matter, such as stones and sand, that is carried onto land or into the water by wind, water, or land movement

volcanic eruption: the bursting forth of hot, liquid rock from within the earth

FOR MORE INFORMATION

Books

Pellant, Chris. *The Best Book of Fossils, Rocks, and Minerals.* New York, NY: Kingfisher Publications, 2007.

Spilsbury, Richard, and Louise Spilsbury. *Fossils.* Chicago, IL: Heinemann Library, 2011.

Websites

Petrified Forest National Park for Kids
www.nps.gov/pefo/forkids/index.htm
Watch a video about the park, and learn how to become a junior ranger.

WebRangers
www.nps.gov/webrangers/
Learn how the National Park Service takes care of parks.

INDEX